Guide to Pacific Northwest Wines:
Whatcom, Skagit, Island & Snohomish County

Vintners Passport

©2017

Dilettante Living Press

Cover Image Credits:

Mt. Baker, Used under CC0 license, Public Domain

Wine Glass, Used under CC0 license, Public Domain

Grape Vines, Used under CC0 license, Public Domain

A special thanks to all the winemakers who took time away from the vines to speak with us for this book.

Table of Contents

INTRODUCTION 1

PUGET SOUND AVA 3

WHATCOM COUNTY: WINERIES 7

SKAGIT COUNTY: WINERIES 19

ISLAND COUNTY: WINERIES 30

SNOHOMISH COUNTY: WINERIES 45

TASTING TIPS 60

THANK YOU 65

MORE WINES… 66

Introduction

Welcome to your passport to regional wine tasting. This series was conceived to accomplish a few things:

1. Focus on regional wine tasting rather than entire states

2. Keep wine tasting affordable—we let you know the starting price of a bottle so you can decide if it is in your comfort zone. We've excluded wineries whose prices start at over $30.

3. Foster connections with the people making wine by including interviews with wine makers.

4. Give you space to take notes as you taste. Yes, we encourage you to write in this book! It is meant to be part guide book, part wine journal.

The information in this book was accurate to the best of our knowledge at the time of publication. Wineries may close, move, sell out of your favorite wine, or change their prices after a book is published. Many of the wineries in this region are small, and as such you should double check their website for seasonal business hours. Some wineries double as wedding venues or may be booked for an event. It can be wise to call ahead.

You can also find these wineries on our website,
www.vintnerspassport.com

Puget Sound AVA

The Puget Sound AVA extends from west of the Cascade mountains to the Pacific Ocean. In the north, it flanks the Canadian border and extends as far south as Olympia.

This guide and tasting journal covers the northern half of the Puget Sound AVA—Whatcom, Skagit, Island, and Snohomish counties.

Many people dismiss the Puget Sound as unsuitable for grape growing due to its cold, rainy climate many months of the year. It's not all rain though--the area has dry summers with moderate temperatures. The grapes that grow well here are usually early ripening varietals.

Many wineries located in the western part of the state source their grapes from the vineyards of eastern Washington where conditions are much hotter. Yet, there are wineries in the region using estate grown varietals such as Madeleine Angevine, Muller Thurgau, Siegerrebe, and Pinot Noir. White varietals tend to be favored for estate grown wines and are often similar to those grown in northern Europe (especially Germany).

Muller Thurgau was developed in the late 1800's as a cross between Riesling and Madeleine Royale. The intent was to create a grape that would ripen earlier. It was very popular in Germany up until the 1980's. Being at a similar latitude to southern Germany, as well as having short summers, makes this grape an ideal choice for the Pacific Northwest region. Muller Thurgau produces a white wine that wine snobs consider flat and uninteresting. This is unfair though, and likely stems back to its reputation as a mass produced German wine in the 20th century. Puget Sound wineries are using it to create a dry, crisp white with nice sweetness.

Madeleine Angevine is another early ripening grape that has its parentage in Madeleine Royale. It grows well in cool climates, making it an attractive choice for Puget Sound growers. It pairs well with seafood, which is convenient in a wine region that abuts the Pacific Ocean. It is described as crisp, floral, grassy, dry, with hints of melon and peach.

Siegerrebe is yet another grape with German ancestry, this time a cross between Madeleine Angevine and Gewurztraminer. This varietal is found growing in areas of Washington and British Columbia. Its flavors and aromas tend to echo its parentage and it makes a nice low acid wine that is fruity and fragrant. It is often blended with other grapes.

Pinot Noir is one of the very few reds that are estate grown in the Puget Sound AVA. The Washington State University extension in the Skagit Valley tested a few cultivars of Pinot Noir years ago, and as a result you can now find some estate grown Pinot Noir in the region. Generally, the northern part of the appellation is not as warm as the southern part of the AVA, making it a bit finicky to grow successfully.

Planning your visit:

Tasting the wines in this region is a treat. As you escape the bustle of the Seattle area tasting rooms, you will find idyllic settings and small, friendly tasting rooms in this largely agricultural region.

The San Juan Islands boast a handful of wineries, but beware that on most islands you will need a car to get where you are going. The state ferry system services the islands throughout the day. Whidbey Island can be reached by car from the north, or by ferry from the south. All other regions are on the mainland.

Besides wine, the area boasts craft breweries and distilleries, cheesemakers and other artisans. There are also great towns for strolling and dining. Notable areas include:

- The Fairhaven district of Bellingham, as well as the downtown public market.
- La Conner in Skagit County

- Friday Harbor on San Juan Island
- The town of Snohomish in Snohomish County
- The town of Langley on Whidbey Island

Tasting Fees:

Most of the wineries in this region have very reasonable tasting fees. Tastings for $5 are typical, but may extend up to $10, making it a bargain in comparison to more popular wine regions. Some wineries also sell by the flight or by the glass, and many will waive the fee with a wine purchase.

Special Events:

Red Wine and Chocolate (February)

Various locations throughout Washington

Snohomish Wine Festival (March)

www.snohomishcoc.com/WineFestival/

Anacortes Spring Wine Festival (April)

www.anacortes.org/spring-wine-festival/

Whidbey Island:

Savor Spring (May)

Autumn on Whidbey (November)

www.whidbeyislandvintners.org/events

Bellingham Northwest Wine Festival (August)

www.bellinghamnorthwestwinefestival.com

Savor the San Juans (September -November)

www.visitsanjuans.com/savor

Skagit Wine and Beer Festival (November)

www.mountvernonchamber.com/events/annual-chamber-events/skagit-wine-festival/

Whatcom County: Wineries

Coach House Cellars

1319 11th St.
Bellingham, WA 98226
Website: www.coachhousecellars.com
Phone: (360) 306-8794

Hours: Monday-Thursday 10:00 am – 7:00 pm; Friday-Saturday 10:00 am-9:00 pm; Sunday 10:00 am – 6:00 pm

Wines start at: $13
Varietals: Chardonnay, Merlot, Cabernet Sauvignon, Syrah

Varietal_____Year_____

Appearance_____

Aroma _____

Taste_____

_____

Price_____My Rating_____

Varietal_____Year_____

Appearance_____

Aroma _____

Taste_____

_____

Price_____My Rating_____

Dynasty Cellars

2169 E. Bakerview Rd.
Bellingham, WA 98226
Website: www.dynastycellars.com
Phone: (360) 758-2958

Hours: Thursdays through Saturdays 1:00 to 6:00 pm; Sundays 1:00 to 4:00 pm

Wines start at: $15
Varietals: Riesling, Malbec, Cabernet Sauvignon, Merlot, Zinfandel, Syrah, Red Blends, Late Harvest Zinfandel

Varietal_____Year_____
Appearance_____
Aroma _____
Taste_____
_____
Price_____My Rating_____

Varietal_____Year_____
Appearance_____
Aroma _____
Taste_____
_____
Price_____My Rating_____

Glm Wine Co.

1678 Boblett St.
Blaine, WA 98230
Website: www.glmwine.com
Phone: (360) 332-2097

Hours: Saturdays 12:00 to 6:00; Sundays 12:00 to 5:00

Wines start at: $12
Varietals: Chardonnay, Rose, Gamay Noir, Cabernet Sauvignon, Red Blend

Varietal_____Year_____

Appearance_____

Aroma _____

Taste_____

_____

Price_____My Rating_____

Varietal_____Year_____

Appearance_____

Aroma _____

Taste_____

_____

Price_____My Rating_____

Honeymoon Mead & Cider

1053 North State St Alley
Bellingham, WA 98225
Website: www.honeymoonmeads.com
Phone: (360) 734-0728

Hours: Tuesday-Saturday 5:00 pm to 11:00 pm
Enjoy appetizers, desserts and live music in their all ages public house

Wines start at: $15
Varietals: Mead, Wassail, Fruit Meads, Apple Cider, Fruit Apple Ciders

Varietal_____Year_____

Appearance_____

Aroma _____

Taste_____

_____

Price_____My Rating_____

Varietal_____Year_____

Appearance_____

Aroma _____

Taste_____

_____

Price_____My Rating_____

Inyo Vineyard and Winery

3337 Agate Heights Rd.
Bellingham, WA 98226
Website: www.inyowine.com
Phone: (360) 647-0441

Hours: Fridays 12:00 to 5:00 pm

Varietals: Riesling, Madeleine Angevine-Siegerrebe, Sangiovese-Barbera, Syrah, Syrah-Mouvedre, Red Blend

Varietal_____Year_____

Appearance_____

Aroma _____

Taste_____

_____

Price_____My Rating_____

Varietal_____Year_____

Appearance_____

Aroma _____

Taste_____

_____

Price_____My Rating_____

Legoe Bay Winery

4232 Legoe Bay Rd.
Lummi Island, WA 98262
Website: www.legoebaywinery.com
Phone: (360) 758-9992
Note: Requires a short ferry ride to get to Lummi Island

Hours: Saturdays and Sundays 1:00 pm to 6:00 pm

Wines start at: $14
Varietals: Pinot Gris, Chardonnay, Orange Muscat, Syrah, Red Blend, Petit Verdot, Malbec

Varietal_____Year_____
Appearance_____
Aroma _____
Taste_____
_____
Price_____My Rating_____

Varietal_____Year_____
Appearance_____
Aroma _____
Taste_____
_____
Price_____My Rating_____

Masquerade Wine Co.

3950 Hammer Drive, Ste. 101
Bellingham WA 98226
Website: www.masqueradewines.com
Phone: (360) 220-7072

Hours: Daily 11:00 am to 6:00 pm

Wines start at: $14
Varietals: Pinot Gris, Viognier, Syrah, Tempranillo, Pinot Noir, Malbec, Barbera, Cabernet Sauvignon, Rousanne, Chenin Blanc, Chardonnay, White and Red late harvest dessert wines, sparkling Lemberger, Riesling, and Moscato, Brut Sparkling wine, Gewürztraminer, Merlot, Cabernet Franc

Varietal_____Year_____

Appearance_____

Aroma _____

Taste_____

_____

Price_____My Rating_____

Varietal_____Year_____

Appearance_____

Aroma _____

Taste_____

_____

Price_____My Rating_____

Mt. Baker Vineyards

4298 Mt. Baker Highway
Everson, WA 98247
Website: www.mountbakervineyards.com
Phone: (360) 592-2300

Hours: Daily 12:00 to 5:00 pm

Wines start at: $14
Types: Whites, Reds, Fruit, Dessert, Sparkling
Varietals: Chardonnay, Madeleine Angevine, Muller-Thurgau, Pinot Gris, Riesling, Siegerrebe, Cabernet Franc, Cabernet Sauvignon, Syrah, Malbec, Merlot, Petit Verdot, Pinot Noir, Sangiovese, Tempranillo, Red Blend, Brut Sparkling Wine, Plum Wine, Apple Wine, Late Harvest Pinot Gris

Varietal_____Year_____
Appearance_____
Aroma _____
Taste_____
_____
Price_____My Rating_____

Varietal_____Year_____
Appearance_____
Aroma _____
Taste_____
_____
Price_____My Rating_____

Samson Estates Winery

1861 Van Dyk Rd.
Everson, WA 98247
Website: www.samsonestates.com
Phone: (360) 966-7787

Hours: Vary by season-please check website. Friday through Sunday 11:00 am to 5:00 pm in spring; Daily 11:00 am to 6:00 am in summer; closed holidays

Wines start at: $12
Varietals: Chardonnay, Riesling, Syrah, Merlot, Raspberry, Blackberry, Blueberry, Raspberry Dessert Wine, Hazelnut Dessert Wine, Blackcurrant Port, Blueberry Dessert Wine

What is your goal with your winemaking?
Our goal is to provide high quality and unique wines at affordable prices. We also like to feature the berry and dessert wines based on our regional high-quality berry crops.

What are your most popular wines with guests?
Our three most popular wines are Delilah Raspberry fruit wine, Cassis (black currant port wine), and Oro (hazelnut dessert wine)

What wine(s) are you most proud of?
Our fruit wines and dessert/port wines are made from the fruit we grow on our own estates and we take special pride in them

What makes a visit to Samson Estate's special?
Our winery is set amid beautiful mountain scenery and our grounds feature sweeping lawns, perennial gardens, a rustic tasting room with summer seating under the eaves, and an attractive outdoor event pavilion. In the summer, we are open 7 days a week from 11 am until 6pm and we host many family and special events at our winery.

Varietal_____Year_____

Appearance_____

Aroma _____

Taste_____

_____

Price_____My Rating_____

Varietal_____Year_____

Appearance_____

Aroma _____

Taste_____

_____

Price_____My Rating_____

Varietal_____Year_____

Appearance_____

Aroma _____

Taste_____

_____

Price_____My Rating_____

Varietal_____Year_____

Appearance_____

Aroma _____

Taste_____

_____

Price_____My Rating_____

Vartanyan Estate Winery

1628 Huntley Rd.
Bellingham WA 98226
Website: www.vewinery.com
Phone: (360) 756-6770

Hours: Fridays through Sundays, 1:00 to 5:00 (6:00 on Saturdays)

Wines start at: $14
Varietals: Riesling, Chardonnay, White Blend, Red Blend, Merlot, Cabernet Sauvignon, Syrah, Cabernet Franc, Tempranillo, Nebbiolo

Varietal_____Year_____

Appearance_____

Aroma _____

Taste_____

_____

Price_____My Rating_____

Varietal_____Year_____

Appearance_____

Aroma _____

Taste_____

_____

Price_____My Rating_____

Skagit County: Wineries

Bertelsen Winery

20598 Starbird Rd.
Mt. Vernon, WA 98274
Website: www.bertelsenwinery.com
Phone: (360) 445-2300

Hours: Wednesday 2:00 to 6:00 pm; Thursday –Saturday 12:00 to 8:00 pm; Sunday 12:00 to 6:00 pm
Tasting fee: $5, waived with purchase

Wines start at: $18
Varietals: Riesling, Chardonnay, Merlot, Syrah, Cabernet Franc, Cabernet Sauvignon

Varietal_____Year_____

Appearance_____

Aroma _____

Taste_____

_____

Price_____My Rating_____

Varietal_____Year_____

Appearance_____

Aroma _____

Taste_____

_____

Price_____My Rating_____

Carpenter Creek Winery

20376 E. Hickox Rd.
Mount Vernon, WA 98274
Website: www.carpentercreek.com
Phone: (360) 708-0700

Hours: Saturday-Sunday 11:00 am to 6:00 pm

Wines start at: $12.50
Varietals: Pinot Noir, Lemberger, Red Blend, Malbec, Merlot, Syrah, Cabernet Sauvignon, Pinot Gris, Albarino, Chardonnay, Viognier, Siegerrebe, Riesling, Rose, Late Harvest Viognier, Late Harvest Pinot Gris

Varietal_____Year_____
Appearance_____
Aroma _____
Taste_____
_____
Price_____My Rating_____

Varietal_____Year_____
Appearance_____
Aroma _____
Taste_____
_____
Price_____My Rating_____

Eagle Haven Winery

8243 Sims Road
Sedro-Woolley, WA 98284
Website: www.eaglehavenwinery.com
Phone: (360) 856-6248

Hours: Fridays 2:00 to 7:00 pm; Saturday-Sunday 11:00 AM to 6:00 pm

Wines start at: $14
Varietals: Siegerrebe, Madeleine Angevine, White Blend, Rose, Pinot Noir, Tempranillo, Cabernet Sauvignon, Apple, Pear

Varietal_____Year_____

Appearance_____

Aroma _____

Taste_____

_____

Price_____My Rating_____

Varietal_____Year_____

Appearance_____

Aroma _____

Taste_____

_____

Price_____My Rating_____

Glacier Peak Winery

58575 State Route 20
Rockport, WA 98283
Website: www.glacierpeakwines.com
Phone: (360) 873-4073; Mt. Vernon tasting room (360) 419-9107

Hours: Friday-Monday 12:00 pm to 6:00 pm

Wines start at: $14
Varietals: Siegerrebe, Gewürztraminer, Madeleine Angevine, Pinot Noir, Syrah, Merlot, Cabernet Sauvignon, Malbec, Black Currant, Blueberry, and Raspberry Dessert wine, Apple pie liqueur

Varietal_____Year_____
Appearance_____
Aroma _____
Taste_____
_____
Price_____My Rating_____

Varietal_____Year_____
Appearance_____
Aroma _____
Taste_____
_____
Price_____My Rating_____

Silver Bell Winery

1724 E. RioVista Ave.
Burlington, WA 98233
Website: www.silverbellwinery.com
Phone: (360) 757-9463

Hours: By appointment

Wines start at: $19
Varietals: Red Blend, Miscela Bianco, Syrah, Pinot Gris, Chardonnay, Cabernet Franc, Merlot, Rose, Riesling, Cabernet Sauvignon, Rousanne

Varietal_____Year_____

Appearance_____

Aroma _____

Taste_____

_____

Price_____My Rating_____

Varietal_____Year_____

Appearance_____

Aroma _____

Taste_____

_____

Price_____My Rating_____

Tulip Valley Vineyard & Orchard

16163 State Route 536
Mount Vernon, WA
Website: www.tulipvalley.net
Phone: (360) 428-6894

Hours: Varies: Friday through Sunday 11 am to 5:00 pm (May through September); extended hours during April (Tulip Festival)

Varietals: Red Blend, Riesling, Gewurtraminer, Pinot Noir, Rose, Apple Cider, Pear Cider

Varietal_____Year_____
Appearance_____
Aroma _____
Taste_____
_____
Price_____My Rating_____

Varietal_____Year_____
Appearance_____
Aroma _____
Taste_____
_____
Price_____My Rating_____

Pasek Cellars

18729 Fir Island Rd.
Mount Vernon, WA 98273
Website: www.pasekcellars.com
Phone: (360) 445-4048

Hours: Daily 11:00 am to 5:00 pm

Wines start at: $12
Varietals: Chardonnay, Muscat Cannelli, Blackberry, Blueberry, Cranberry, Loganberry, Raspberry, Passion Fruit, Pineapple, Syrah Port, Red Blend, Fruit Dessert Wines: Raspberry, Blackberry; Coffee Dessert Wine

What is your mission/goal with your wines?
Our mission is to please people. Many people want to like wine but don't like the typical dry taste and are confused by reviews comparing the taste of wine to things like pencil lead, cigar box and cream corn. Our wines are fresh, straight forward and true to the fruit. If you like a fruit, you'll like the wine we make from it.

What are your 3 most popular wines?
Cranberry wine is our most popular. This is driven by sales during the holidays but it is available and loved by many all year. The wine is made from whole cranberries grown in Grayland, WA. We use Oregon blackberries to make our second most popular wine, blackberry wine. Raspberry Wine and Passion fruit wine are similar in sales and essentially tied for third.

What wine are you most proud of (and why)? I am most proud of Cranberry wine because it has reached the most people. We distribute this wine in 16 states. It has become a holiday tradition for many families.

What makes a visit to your winery special?
While most of our wines are sweet we have a few nice dry wines. The wines will please everyone, even non-wine drinkers.

Varietal_____Year_____
Appearance_____
Aroma _____
Taste_____

_____

Price_____My Rating_____

Varietal_____Year_____
Appearance_____
Aroma _____
Taste_____

_____

Price_____My Rating_____

Varietal_____Year_____
Appearance_____
Aroma _____
Taste_____

_____

Price_____My Rating_____

Varietal_____Year_____
Appearance_____
Aroma _____
Taste_____

_____

Price_____My Rating_____

Skagit Cellars

128 S 1st Street
LaConner, WA 98257
Website: www.skagitcellars.com
Phone: (360) 708-2801

Hours: Saturday-Sunday 12:00 pm to 6:00 pm

Wines start at: $22
Varietals: Viognier, Pinot Gris, Cabernet Sauvignon, Malbec, Raspberry Chocolate Port

What is your mission/goal with your wines?
To provide great quality wine, great service and have fun!

What are your 3 most popular wines?
Cabernet Sauvignon, Malbec, Pinot Gris

What wine are you most proud of (and why)?
Hard to narrow it down to one. Likely the Pinot Gris & the Malbec since they were just awarded an International Silver Medal! That makes us proud.

What makes a visit to your winery special?
Great location in a "go-to" city of La Conner. Located on the Channel!

Varietal_____Year_____

Appearance_____

Aroma _____

Taste_____

_____

Price_____My Rating_____

Varietal_____Year_____

Appearance_____

Aroma _____

Taste_____

_____

Price_____My Rating_____

Varietal_____Year_____

Appearance_____

Aroma _____

Taste_____

_____

Price_____My Rating_____

Varietal_____Year_____

Appearance_____

Aroma _____

Taste_____

_____

Price_____My Rating_____

Island County: Wineries

Comforts of Whidbey

5219 View Rd.
Langley, WA 98260
Website: www.comfortsofwhidbey.com
Phone: (360) 969-2961

Hours: Thursday-Monday 12:00 to 5:00 pm (Seasonal)

Varietals: Madeleine Sylvaner, Madeleine Angevine, Siegerrebe, White Blend, Sangiovese, Syrah, Cabernet Sauvignon, Malbec, Late Harvest Viognier

Varietal_____Year_____
Appearance_____
Aroma _____
Taste_____
_____
Price_____My Rating_____

Varietal_____Year_____
Appearance_____
Aroma _____
Taste_____
_____
Price_____My Rating_____

Blooms Winery

5603 Bayview Rd.
Langley, WA 98260
Website: www.bloomswinery.com
Phone: (360) 321-0515

Hours: Monday-Thursday 1:00-6:00 pm; Friday 1:00-8:00 pm; Saturdays 11:00 am – 6:00 pm; Sundays 12:00 pm-6:00 pm

Wines start at: $14
Varietals: Cabernet Sauvignon, Red Blend, Syrah, Petit Verdot, Malbec, Merlot, Rose, Port, White Blend, Viognier, Semillon, Riesling, Sauvignon Blanc, Pinot Gris, Semillon Dessert Wine, Rhubarb

What is your mission with your wines?
Our mission is simply to create the best wines we can. Creating fine wines, one at a time. Small lots with attention to detail, helps establish consistently fine quality.

What are your three most popular wines?
Our most popular dry white is our Viognier, although we have 6 to choose from and they split pretty evenly. The reds are even harder to pinpoint one or two--our top blend is the Poetic (double gold medal Seattle Wine Awards, selected as a top pick by Washington Tasting Room magazine) and our Syrah or Cabernet are probably our top selling varietals. We also have a sweeter white - our Beach Cabin blend that is very popular (again, double gold medal Seattle Wine Awards).

Which wine are you most proud of and why?
The Poetic is our favorite and is a blend of Malbec, Syrah and Petit Verdot. The current release of Poetic is about 50% Syrah, 40% Malbec and 10% Petit Verdot. It's a wonderful blend, always rich, flavorful and complex.

What makes a visit to your winery special?
We are very casual, open to help from friends and fans, and that gives the business a nice 'community' feel. We have an off-site tasting room that is a very comfortable spot for people to sit (we have tables and chairs) and enjoy wine, food (small plates food service with organic cheeses, humus, bruschetta etc.) beer and cider (and non-alcoholic), plus live music a couple of times a week. We have a great deck to enjoy the outside, and always have local artists work showing and for sale.

Varietal_____Year_____

Appearance_____

Aroma _____

Taste_____

_____

Price_____My Rating_____

Varietal_____Year_____

Appearance_____

Aroma _____

Taste_____

_____

Price_____My Rating_____

Varietal_____Year_____

Appearance_____

Aroma _____

Taste_____

_____

Price_____My Rating_____

Dancing Fish Vineyards

1953 Newman Road
Freeland, WA 98249
Website: www.dancingfishvineyards.com
Phone: (425) 503-7655

Hours: Thursday & Sunday 11:00 to 4:00 pm; Fridays 12:00 to 6:00 pm; Saturdays 11:00 to 5:00 pm

Wines start at: $26
Varietals: Chardonnay, Sauvignon Blanc, Red Blends, Merlot, Cabernet Sauvignon, Syrah

Varietal_____Year_____
Appearance_____
Aroma _____
Taste_____
_____
Price_____My Rating_____

Varietal_____Year_____
Appearance_____
Aroma _____
Taste_____
_____
Price_____My Rating_____

Holmes Harbor Cellars

4591 Honeymoon Bay Rd.
Greenbank, WA 98253
Website: www.holmesharborcellars.com
Phone: (360) 331-3544

Hours: Wednesday – Sunday 12:00 to 6:00 pm

Wines start at: $18
Varietals: White Blend, Riesling, Merlot, Cabernet Sauvignon, Malbec, Red Blend, Syrah, Petit Verdot, Viognier, Zinfandel, Tempranillo, Semillon, Port, Late Harvest Zinfandel

Varietal_____Year_____
Appearance_____
Aroma _____
Taste_____
_____
Price_____My Rating_____

Varietal_____Year_____
Appearance_____
Aroma _____
Taste_____
_____
Price_____My Rating_____

Lopez Island Vineyards

265 Lopez Road
Lopez Village, WA
Website: www.lopezislandvineyards.com
Phone: (360) 468-3644
Note: Requires a ferry ride to get to

Hours: By reservation

Wines start at: $18
Varietals: Madeleine Angevine, Siegerrebe, Sangiovese, Malbec, Cabernet Sauvignon, Port, White Blend, Chardonnay, Rose, Merlot, Raspberry

What is your goal or mission with your wines?
To provide the fresh expression of local vineyards and eastern Washington area

What are your three most popular wines?
Madeleine Angevine, Siegerrebe, Sangiovese

What wine are you personally most proud of and why?
Madeleine Angevine and Siegerrebe. These two we grow ourselves and they are certified organic.

What makes a visit to your winery or the region special?
The area is special because of the weather. The climate allows the wines to reach a level of quality which is unique.

Varietal_____Year_____

Appearance_____

Aroma _____

Taste_____

_____

Price_____My Rating_____

Varietal_____Year_____

Appearance_____

Aroma _____

Taste_____

_____

Price_____My Rating_____

Varietal_____Year_____

Appearance_____

Aroma _____

Taste_____

_____

Price_____My Rating_____

Varietal_____Year_____

Appearance_____

Aroma _____

Taste_____

_____

Price_____My Rating_____

Orcas Island Winery

2371 Crow Valley Road
Eastsound, WA
Website: www.orcasislandwinery.com
Phone: (425) 314-7509
Note: Requires a ferry ride to get to

Hours: Thursday-Sunday 12:00 pm – 6:00 pm (5 pm Sundays)

Wines start at: $18
Varietals: Riesling, Chardonnay, Rose, Cabernet Sauvignon, Cabernet Franc, Merlot, Syrah, Red Blend

Varietal_____Year_____

Appearance_____

Aroma _____

Taste_____

_____

Price_____My Rating_____

Varietal_____Year_____

Appearance_____

Aroma _____

Taste_____

_____

Price_____My Rating_____

Ott & Murphy

204 First St.
Langley, WA 98260
Website: www.ottmurphywines.com
Phone: (360) 221-7131

Hours: Sunday-Thursday (except Wednesday) 1:00 to 8:00 pm; Friday and Saturday 12:00 to 10:00 pm

Wines start at: $19
Varietals: White Blend, Viognier, Counoise, Mourvedre, Tempranillo, Syrah, Malbec, Grenache, Marsanne, Rousanne

Varietal_____Year_____
Appearance_____
Aroma _____
Taste_____
_____
Price_____My Rating_____

Varietal_____Year_____
Appearance_____
Aroma _____
Taste_____
_____
Price_____My Rating_____

San Juan Cellars

2 Cannery Landing
Friday Harbor, WA 98250
Website: www.sanjuancellars.com
Phone: 1-800-248-WINE
Note: Requires a ferry ride to get to

Hours: Daily, 10:00 am – 5:00 pm

Wines start at: $10
Varietals: Sauvignon Blanc, Chardonnay, Pinot Gris, Riesling, Blush, Merlot, Cabernet Sauvignon, Syrah, Moscato, Red blend

Varietal_____Year_____
Appearance_____
Aroma _____
Taste_____
_____
Price_____My Rating_____

Varietal_____Year_____
Appearance_____
Aroma _____
Taste_____
_____
Price_____My Rating_____

San Juan Vineyards

3136 Roche Harbor Rd.
Friday Harbor, WA 98250
Website: www.sanjuanvineyards.com:
Phone: (360) 378-9463
Note: Requires a ferry ride to get to

Hours: 11:00 am – 5:00 pm (Seasonal)

Wines start at: $14
Varietals: Chardonnay, Pinot Gris, Siegerrebe, Madeleine Angevine, Riesling, White blend, Rose, Merlot, Cabernet Sauvignon, Cabernet Franc, Red blend

Varietal_____Year_____
Appearance_____
Aroma _____
Taste_____
_____
Price_____My Rating_____

Varietal_____Year_____
Appearance_____
Aroma _____
Taste_____
_____
Price_____My Rating_____

Whidbey Island Winery

5237 Langley Rd.
Langley, WA 98260
Website: www.whidbeyislandwinery.com
Phone: (360) 221-2040

Hours: Summer: 11:00 am to 5:00 pm except Tuesday; Winter 11:00 am to 5:00 pm except Mondays and Tuesdays

Wines start at: $14
Varietals: White Blend, Madeleine Angevine, Pinot Gris, Rosato, Rousanne, Siegerrebe, Port, Red blend, Cabernet Franc, Dolcetto, Grenache, Lemberger, Malbec, Merlot, Nebbiolo, Pinot Noir, Primitivo, Sangiovese, Syrah

What is your mission with your wines?
We produce a wide variety of wines from grapes grown both here on the cool side of the state and from select vineyards on the warm dry eastern side of the Cascade Mountains. My goal is wines of balance and elegance, in the European tradition, expressing everything the fruit has to offer from both terroir and vintage.

What are your three most popular wine?
Island White (a blend built around 2 of our estate varieties Madeleine Angevine and Madeleine Sylvaner), Sangiovese, and Cabernet Franc

What wine are you most proud of and why?
Island White. A completely proprietary blend from 2 relatively unknown grapes grown in a perhaps unlikely place that has been our sales leader by a wide margin for all of our 25 years of production.

What makes a visit to your winery special?
We are located in an area of stunning natural beauty on the largest of the Puget Sound islands. The winery grounds feature vineyard views, ancient apple trees, abundant wildlife and the best wine around.

Varietal_____Year_____
Appearance_____
Aroma _____
Taste_____

_____

Price_____My Rating_____

Varietal_____Year_____
Appearance_____
Aroma _____
Taste_____

_____

Price_____My Rating_____

Varietal_____Year_____
Appearance_____
Aroma _____
Taste_____

_____

Price_____My Rating_____

Varietal_____Year_____
Appearance_____
Aroma _____
Taste_____

_____

Price_____My Rating_____

Spoiled Dog Winery

5881 Maxwelton Rd.
Langley, WA 98260
Website: www.spoileddogwinery.com
Phone: (360) 661-6226

Hours: Saturday & Sunday 12:00 to 5:00 pm or by appointment

Wines start at: $15
Varietals: Pinot Gris, Sauvignon Blanc, Rose, Apple wine, Lavender Verjus, Merlot, Pinot Noir, Malbec, Red blend,

Varietal_____Year_____

Appearance_____

Aroma _____

Taste_____

_____

Price_____My Rating_____

Varietal_____Year_____

Appearance_____

Aroma _____

Taste_____

_____

Price_____My Rating_____

Snohomish County: Wineries

Dubindil Winery

1311 Bonneville Ave. Suite 105
Snohomish, WA 98290
Website: www.dubindilwinery.com
Phone: (360) 453-7352

Hours: By appointment

Wines start at: $19
Varietals: Red blend, Cabernet Sauvignon

Varietal_____Year_____

Appearance_____

Aroma _____

Taste_____

_____

Price_____My Rating_____

Varietal_____Year_____

Appearance_____

Aroma _____

Taste_____

_____

Price_____My Rating_____

Dusty Cellars

529 Michael Way
Camano Island, WA 98282
Website: www.dustycellarswinery.com
Phone: (360) 387-2729

Hours: First weekend of the month; call for group reservations

Wines start at: $15
Varietals: Cabernet Franc, Merlot, Syrah, Malbec

Varietal_____Year_____
Appearance_____
Aroma _____
Taste_____
_____
Price_____My Rating_____

Varietal_____Year_____
Appearance_____
Aroma _____
Taste_____
_____
Price_____My Rating_____

Edward Lynne Cellars

748 Vineyard Ln
Camano Island, WA 98282
Website: www.elcellars.webs.com
Phone: (360) 929-6072

Hours: Summers-first weekend of the month 12:00 – 5:00 pm; special events

Varietals: Siegerrebe, Madeleine Angevine, Riesling, Red blend, Merlot, Cabernet Sauvignon

Varietal_____Year_____
Appearance_____
Aroma _____
Taste_____
_____
Price_____My Rating_____

Varietal_____Year_____
Appearance_____
Aroma _____
Taste_____
_____
Price_____My Rating_____

Furion Cellars

1311 Bonneville Ave, Suite 106
Website: www.furioncellars.com
Phone: (425) 314-8922

Hours: By appointment

Wines start at: $21
Varietals: Sangiovese, Red Blend, Cabernet Sauvignon, Syrah

Varietal_____Year_____
Appearance_____
Aroma _____
Taste_____
_____

Price_____My Rating_____

Varietal_____Year_____
Appearance_____
Aroma _____
Taste_____
_____

Price_____My Rating_____

Gregarious Cellars

19414 208th Ave SE
Monroe, Washington
No Website
Phone: (425) 691-0504

Hours: Seasonal, Saturdays-Sundays 12:00 pm – 5:00 pm

Wines start at: $15
Varietals: Rosato, Red blend, Syrah, Cabernet Sauvignon, Semillon

Varietal_____Year_____
Appearance_____
Aroma _____
Taste_____
_____
Price_____My Rating_____

Varietal_____Year_____
Appearance_____
Aroma _____
Taste_____
_____
Price_____My Rating_____

Lantz Cellars

3001 South Lake Stevens Road
Lake Stevens WA 98258
Website: www.lantzcellars.com
Phone: (425) 770-2599

Hours: Contact-open to the public for events

Wines start at: $22
Varietals: White blend, Cabernet Sauvignon, Tempranillo, Syrah, Red blend, Port

Varietal_____Year_____
Appearance_____
Aroma _____
Taste_____
_____
Price_____My Rating_____

Varietal_____Year_____
Appearance_____
Aroma _____
Taste_____
_____
Price_____My Rating_____

Kasia Winery

905 First St.
Snohomish, WA 98290
Website: www.kasiawinery.com
Phone: (425) 941-0224

Hours: Wednesday, Thursday, Sunday 12:00 to 5:00 pm; Friday-Saturday 12:00 to 6:00 pm

Wine start at: $18
Varietals: Rose, Syrah, Mouvedre

What is your mission/goal with your wines?
Surrounded by so many great Washington wineries, I knew from the start that my wines would have to be refined and superbly crafted to meet or exceed the high level of wineries around me.
My goal is to capture the memorable yield of each harvest season in a bottle, blend my love of creating with the art of making unforgettable wines that are meticulously crafted and deeply personal.

What are your 3 most popular wines?
"Open Highway" 100% Red Mountain Syrah, "Off the Hook" Rose, and "Moxie" 100% Mourvèdre

What wine are you most proud of (and why)?
My Red Mountain Syrah. It is first wine I made under my own label. My wines are made from grapes from Red Mountain, which is one of the most acclaimed AVAs in Washington.
I have a different approach to winemaking. I see this as fine art, a special craft that takes time, patience and knowing what your end goal is. I like an old-world approach. I don't like to mess with the wine too much, I want the fruit and the terroir to shine. I take winemaking very personally. I never want to lose the handcrafted aspect and that's why my production is limited.

What makes a visit to your winery special?
When you visit my tasting room you get to meet me as I am here every day getting to know my customers and club members! Also, we have great variety of merchandise in our winery boutique.

Varietal_____Year_____

Appearance_____

Aroma _____

Taste_____

Price_____My Rating_____

Varietal_____Year_____

Appearance_____

Aroma _____

Taste_____

Price_____My Rating_____

Varietal_____Year_____

Appearance_____

Aroma _____

Taste_____

Price_____My Rating_____

King Lake Cellars

22819 King Lake Rd.
Monroe, WA 98272
Website: www.kinglakecellars.com
Phone: (360) 805-5891

Hours: Seasonal; Summers Friday 4:00 to 9:00 pm, Saturdays 12:00 pm – 6:00 pm; Sundays and rest of the year by appointment

Wines start at: $23
Varietals: Sangiovese, Cabernet Sauvignon, Merlot, Syrah, Red blend

What is your mission/goal with your wines?
To create beautiful, hand crafted, boutique wines that are also attainable. Our winemaker invests in high quality grapes and strives to let them showcase their true essence by minimizing the manipulation so common in high production factory wines.

What are your 3 most popular wines?
Our Cabernet, our Red Blend and our Merlot.

What wine are you most proud of (and why)?
Our 2014 Cabernet Franc because it was a late harvest and the fruit was riper than we prefer, we thought it wouldn't amount to much but we decided not to abandon it, we nurtured it through the process, nudged it along when necessary and the result has turned out to be our most elegant and pleasant wine to date.

What makes a visit to your winery special?
We are striving to provide that countryside destination winery experience without having to drive over the mountains. With over 25 acres of property overlooking the Snoqualmie valley, we offer stunning views of Mt. Rainier, a quiet atmosphere to enjoy wine and a picnic, occasional wood fired pizzas and live music. We currently have a wine cave under construction and will continue to invest in creating a sought-after winery experience only 30 minutes outside of Woodinville.

Varietal_____Year_____

Appearance_____

Aroma _____

Taste_____

_____

Price_____My Rating_____

Varietal_____Year_____

Appearance_____

Aroma _____

Taste_____

_____

Price_____My Rating_____

Varietal_____Year_____

Appearance_____

Aroma _____

Taste_____

_____

Price_____My Rating_____

Varietal_____Year_____

Appearance_____

Aroma _____

Taste_____

_____

Price_____My Rating_____

Port Gardner Bay

3006 Rucker Avenue
Everett WA 98201
Website: www.portgardnerbaywinery.com
Phone: (425) 339-0293

Hours: Thursday-Saturday 4:30 to 10:00 pm

Wines start at: $15
Varietals: Chardonnay, Riesling, Merlot, Cabernet Sauvignon, Malbec, Carmenere, Syrah, Sangiovese, Red Blend, Blueberry blend

Varietal_____Year_____

Appearance_____

Aroma _____

Taste_____

_____

Price_____My Rating_____

Varietal_____Year_____

Appearance_____

Aroma _____

Taste_____

_____

Price_____My Rating_____

VanCamp Cellars

1311 Bonneville Ave. Ste. 104
Snohomish WA 98290
Website: www.vancampcellars.com
Phone: (425) 330-0338

Hours: Saturdays 12:00 to 5:00 pm

Wines start at: $20
Varietals: Red blend, Viognier, Syrah, Merlot, Cabernet Franc, Cabernet Sauvignon

Varietal_____Year_____
Appearance_____
Aroma _____
Taste_____
_____
Price_____My Rating_____

Varietal_____Year_____
Appearance_____
Aroma _____
Taste_____
_____
Price_____My Rating_____

Randolph Cellars

1007 1ˢᵗ St.
Snohomish, WA 98290
Website: www.randolphcellars.com
Phone: (360) 243-3994

Hours: Thursday-Saturday 1:00-7:00 pm; Sundays 1:00-5:00 pm

Wines start at: $18
Varietals: Riesling, Chardonnay, Rose, Cabernet Sauvignon, Merlot, Syrah, Cabernet Franc, Malbec, Mourvedre, Red Blend

What is your mission/goal with your wines?
To make some of the most memorable wines in Washington State and have fun doing it.

What are your 3 most popular wines?
Dry Riesling, Syrah, Petit Verdot

What wine are you most proud of (and why)?
Our 100% Petit Verdot because it is so rarely done and so beautiful when done right.

What makes a visit to your winery special?
We are the first full production Winery and Tasting Room in the historic downtown of Snohomish along the river. It is a quaint little town to hang out and spend a weekend day and it is also an up and coming little wine area with a couple of other tasting rooms.

Varietal_____Year_____

Appearance_____

Aroma _____

Taste_____

Price_____My Rating_____

Varietal_____Year_____

Appearance_____

Aroma _____

Taste_____

Price_____My Rating_____

Varietal_____Year_____

Appearance_____

Aroma _____

Taste_____

Price_____My Rating_____

Varietal_____Year_____

Appearance_____

Aroma _____

Taste_____

Price_____My Rating_____

Tasting Tips

Visiting wineries is more popular than ever, with ambitious wineries opening their doors in almost every state. Tasting wine at the source is inherently social and filled with potential for exciting discoveries to enrich every wine lover's lifestyle. Here are a few tips and guidelines to help you maximize your next tasting experience on the road.

Keep in mind that a good day of tasting wine is usually a marathon for your system. Be sure to bring extra water and always have healthy snacks readily available. Some wineries provide amazing foods for sustenance and food pairing, while others only set out simple crackers or bread to clear your palate.

Planning

Make sure that you know the wineries along your route. It would be a shame to be passionate about Syrah, for example, and later realize that a winery dedicated to making great Syrah was located between your second and third stops.

Double check to see if any target wineries require a reservation. Wine cultures vary dramatically around the world when it comes to opening their doors and receiving guests. Many smaller wineries are happy to share their latest releases, but just don't have the staffing and resources to maintain an open door during business hours.

Think of breakfast as the most important meal of the day. A full stomach when you arrive at your first stop is your best bet for having the energy and stamina for whatever the day brings.

Have a plan for protecting your purchases from the heat of a vehicle. A standard wine box with dividers works great for a few bottles, but make sure to bring plenty of small icepacks to keep your new treasures cool.

Tasting

Tasting wines at a winery is an opportunity to experience passionate winemaking and there are some steps you can take to make sure you get the most out of your experience.

Order

It is true that tasting order is not crucial to enjoying wine, but you can certainly make it easier for your brain to do its job if you follow simple guidelines.

- White wines should come first so that you can appreciate their mineral elements.
- Rose's should follow as they provide a natural transition to reds.
- Dessert wines should always come after table wines since it is much easier to make the transition on the palate from dry to sweet impressions.

You can also order wines within each main group from lighter body to heavier body to gain an even greater tasting efficiency. Fortunately, many wineries have learned to anticipate these concerns and have a suggested tasting order. Don't ever be shy about asking for a reasonable tasting order if it is not clear on the list of available wines.

Colors

Wines of all kinds present explicit and vibrant hues, especially at the edges. Moreover, there is an engaging brightness to both whites and reds that becomes apparent when you hold the glass to the light.

Lighter whites will sometimes have a faint greenish tint, while heavier whites typically show a range of straw and light yellow. White dessert wines have the golden yellow that is normally associated with dry white wines in their prime.

Red wines have a spectrum that runs from light ruby to deep purple. Don't be surprised, though, if some of the heavier reds are downright opaque.

The trickiest wines to evaluate by color are rose's. There is an extremely wide spectrum of pinks and salmons depending on which red grape(s) were used and how much contact with the skins took place.

Aromas

There are no guarantees when your nose encounters wines in a tasting room. Still, there are some general themes that emerge as you taste through a range of wines. Simple wines can be delightfully expressive and complex wines are sometimes quite shy. Be sure to hold your glass flat on the counter and swirl each sample to bring out the aromas and flavors.

White wines usually show some degree of light floral and/or citrus notes. Rose's will almost always smell slightly candied or present fresh strawberry notes. Reds can be more mysterious, particularly in their first year or two in the bottle, so don't be surprised if the aromas of a big, bold Cabernet add up to a wall of vague black fruit. Dessert wines seem dramatic, by comparison, with their apricot and peach notes. Just keep swirling and appreciate whatever interesting notes that the wine is willing to share.

Flavors

Whites and dessert wines tend to be more expressive than roses and reds. This follows, in part, from the common presence of the tannin compounds that are found in red grape skins. They provide the necessary backbone for a full-bodied wine with aging potential, but can also dominate the mouthfeel of the palate in a way that makes it hard to map out specific notes in a flavor profile. Bear in mind that many well-made wines are almost mute when we smell them, but present a wide range of fascinating flavors when you take the time to fully engage the palate.

Rinsing your glass with water between each group or flight of wines is the most reliable way to ensure that you are tasting a wine's correct flavor profile. That's also a great time to clear your palate with simple breads and/or crackers.

Many people would agree that you will encounter very familiar impressions when you taste a range of wines. Lighter bodied whites usually evoke memories of citrus and mild flowers. Heavier whites (including dessert wines) can be much more complex and show off notes of stone fruits such as nectarines and apricots. Rose's and red wines have an even wider spectrum and can present notes of everything from rhubarb to blueberries to blackberries. On top of that, young reds can also have secondary layers of smoky and woodsy notes owing to tannins and oak.

Tasting wines, though, should never feel like a quest for a definitive impression. The real fun comes from letting your brain sort out the magnitude of sensations. For example, a young sauvignon blanc might remind you of limes. That could mean the intensity of a lime after you cut it open, but it could also mean the subtle experience of lime in a key lime pie. There are plenty of experts on winemaking and wine producing regions, but *you* are the only expert on your palate.

Evaluating

Most well-made wines share some critical features. First, look for distinct progress on the palate. A decently made wine should present itself like a three act play with a beginning, a middle and an end. Secondly, there should be some sense of balance between the basic elements of fruit, acid and alcohol. It may be a red flag for a wine's potential if any of these sensations is too dominant on the palate.

Don't forget to keep track of "big picture" impressions to make buying decisions as easy as possible. Simple designations like Yes, No and Maybe ultimately work as well in a tasting room setting as any traditional wine scoring system.

Purchasing

Small purchases usually make the most sense, especially if you have a way to keep the bottles safe and cool throughout the day. For larger purchases, consider having the winery ship the wine home or even joining their wine club to take advantage of discounts and limited releases.

Remember, you can always reward a winery's outstanding hospitality with a gift shop purchase if the wines just don't match your expectations or preferences.

Maximizing Your Experience

It is easy to focus so much on the mechanics of tasting wines that you lose sight of the overall experience. Fortunately, there are two specific things you can do at every winery to become a better taster and consumer.

Most importantly, you can dramatically improve focus and stamina by getting in the habit of spitting out most wines. Staying hydrated with water is helpful, but after swallowing only eight 3-ounce pours you will have effectively consumed an entire bottle of wine. It may be awkward to use a spit bucket, but it is always appropriate to ask for a small plastic cup to keep at the side of your glass.

Next, you can augment your learning curve by availing yourself of the people pouring samples. These fellow wine lovers are intimately familiar with the flavor profiles of their wines. Tasting room staff have usually tasted current vintages with a variety of foods and can provide suggestions for pairing possibilities. Some of these individuals have also had the opportunity to spend time with the winemaker and can give insights into how the wines evolve and perform over time.

Conclusion

Tasting wine at a winery provides a window into a winemaker's efforts to get the most out of specific varietals or even an appellation. Good planning and moderate consumption go a long way toward making a day of tasting a pleasurable and enlightening experience.

Thank you

Thank you for your purchase of this tasting guide and journal. I created this book to scratch my own itch. I wanted a way to keep track of the wines I tasted during my travels that went beyond a blank journal. I hope you will enjoy these "passports" to wine regions.

It can be difficult for independent authors to get noticed. Help from readers is very sincerely appreciated! If you care to, any one of the following would help me spread the word.

- Share this book with your wine loving friends.

- Let us know what region we should cover next (visit us at **www.vintnerspassport.com** and leave a message). While you're there, if there is anything we can improve upon we would love to hear that too.

- Leave a review on your favorite platform. Reviews not only help others know if the book is right for them, but on shopping sites it helps books get found.

- If there is a wine gift shop or local bookstore that you think should carry this book, I would love to hear about it.

More Wines...

Winery_____

Varietal_____Year_____

Appearance_____

Aroma _____

Taste_____

_____

Price_____My Rating_____

Winery_____

Varietal_____Year_____

Appearance_____

Aroma _____

Taste_____

_____

Price_____My Rating_____

Winery_____

Varietal_____Year_____

Appearance_____

Aroma _____

Taste_____

_____

Price_____My Rating_____

Winery_____

Varietal_____Year_____

Appearance_____

Aroma _____

Taste_____

_____

Price_____My Rating_____

Winery_____

Varietal_____Year_____

Appearance_____

Aroma _____

Taste_____

_____

Price_____My Rating_____

Winery_____

Varietal_____Year_____

Appearance_____

Aroma _____

Taste_____

_____

Price_____My Rating_____

Winery_____

Varietal_____Year_____

Appearance_____

Aroma _____

Taste_____

_____

Price_____My Rating_____

Winery_____

Varietal_____Year_____

Appearance_____

Aroma _____

Taste_____

_____

Price_____My Rating_____

Winery_____

Varietal_____Year_____

Appearance_____

Aroma _____

Taste_____

_____

Price_____My Rating_____

www.ingramcontent.com/pod-product-compliance
Lightning Source LLC
Chambersburg PA
CBHW072107290426
44110CB00014B/1857